my house has many windows

poems

sheila rosen

BIG TREE PUBLISHING
LANGLEY, BC

my house has many windows
© Sheila Rosen, 2021
All Rights Reserved, except where otherwise noted
Designed by Patrice Nelson
Published by Big Tree Publishing
Langley, BC Canada
ISBN 978-1-9992463-1-0
www.bigtreepublishing.com

d e d i c a t i o n

These poems are gathered in memory of a house
with thankfulness for my husband Norm
who fitted window after window,
beam after beam into The Cedar House.

Dedicated to my sons and daughters
Carmen Sheila, Russell Norman,
Jay Jonathan, Amanda Jean

and grandchildren
Isaac, Ben, Clara
Tadia, Kezia, Bethany
Amos, Brenna, Maggie, Hendrix
Jaylene, Braden, Aaron, Josiah

who loved The Cedar House

Salish basketry tray c1928, Longworth, east of Prince George, BC

contents

through the cedar door . . .
into the house of many windows

Prologue

10 Cedar, first light
11 I am . . .
12 Old Saying
13 Four Lessons

(I)

16 Clearing Catkins
17 Haiku
17 Yard Guests
18 Stanza
19 Glass
20 Where Paintings Hang
21 I Step Outside
22 Peony Seasons
24 Winged Creatures
25 wisteria god
26 This new world
27 Poppies, front yard
28 May Evening
29 Porch light

(II)

32	Haiku
33	The Boy in the Tree
34	Evenings after others
35	O
36	Bedroom
37	Norm dreams himself out of the woods
38	I like a man
40	dream houses
42	She Comes Into Her Own
44	More Often – a ghazal
45	Tomato Vine
46	Exchange
47	Day of Small Things
48	Intimations of Grace
50	Most of all not water
51	east-facing
52	Afternoon In My Kitchen
53	String theory
54	Windowsill
55	The Glory of the Morning

(III)

58	Haiku
59	Ambulance
60	In The Scattering Season

61	Cottonwood
62	Origami
64	Flicker
65	What The Old Japanese Maple Has To Give
66	Under The Prolific Heavens
67	House Beautiful
68	House, Grumbling
69	Bear's Tooth
70	All
72	Verily (flashback)
73	Mending Basket
74	How We Finish

(IV)

76	Haiku - winter scenes from my study window
77	A Meditation of Crows
78	Back Yard, December
80	Moon-Wine
81	Imagine . . .
82	First Day
83	Crèche
84	Breakable
85	Inventory Fragment
86	Sunset in Real Time
88	Piano Finally Speaks Her Mind

Epilogue

90	Blue Atlas
92	Yellow Pages
93	Tragically Hip
94	Framing the World
95	The Eye Cannot
95	Un Titled
96	The Saffron Gates
98	Lark Ascending
100	Notes and Acknowledgements
101	Previously Published
102	Thank you . . .

prologue

"Home is a truth you carry inside you."

Richard Wagamese

Fijian pine needle basket c1972

Cedar, first light

First light falls on the cedar mask,
one eye-socket, one nostril, two half-lips –
matching parts still night-dark. Dawn
rounds the bend, seeps into concavities
made by the gouge, lights the dark side
of my cedar moon: *Bukwus** –
wild man of the woods.

I sit at table under cedar ceiling,
under *Bukwus* on cedar post. I'm joined
by children and grandchildren, framed
and set on a cedar ledge - my own
small nation, part, of a part, of a nation
set on a continent-edge where cedars
take the wind off the Salish Sea.

I'm child of an English shopkeeper's
boy – turned farmer, miner, logger –
and a red-haired English girl who crossed
that other ocean, that other century.
From cedar post, a cedar countenance,
Bukwus, studies me as I study him.
We are mystery. We are home.

Bertolt Brecht: "I carry a brick on my shoulder, in order that the world may know what my house was like."

I am . . .

(1)
. . . a turtle, I carry my house
on my back. There are many reasons
I grieved when I came to the end
of "Indian Horse" – Wagamese's
book of longing, book of self
and self's wanting, self's home
and home's healing.

(2)
. . . who I am, even without
my round-ish house and the baby-grand
wedding-present piano and the babies
that came, one, two, three, four, all
now in their own surrounds. The cedar house
tended and reflected me, gifts and failings,
its familiar geometry a baseline.
House – akin, maybe, to
land for the first peoples.
The land. It's in the bones. It is ruinous
to remove it from the body.

Old saying

"Leaving is like dying."
A universal wrenching, a rending
for the leaver and the left. We set off
on our dying. With any luck
we have, like Stephen Dedalus,
a mother praying we will learn
what the heart is.

Sibilant whispers – *Aberystwyth*, *Innisfree*,
or *Petra, rose-red city half as old as time.*
Words and names as nectar.

We leave the basement suite
of a nondescript house
in a run-of-the-mill town
where we've stopped a while
on our way to the rose-red city.

A hunger old as time – we follow
what we guess to be our heart.

Four Lessons

"We are always making home" – Shani Mootoo

Home might be the biggest word there is.
Even in happy migrations, I begin to make home,
gather small sticks, bits of straw, downy linings.
In full flight I, at the smallest prompt, become
a nesting bird, a homing pigeon. At sixteen,
I went away, believing home would be
there, waiting, unchanged, for me.
Lesson 1: home can be lost.

It takes time, after loss, to unearth a home – not knowing
what this wanting is. Like the pain you can't describe,
can't pinpoint for the doctor; like driving at night, looking
for a sign, seeing only 'no vacancy'. Aching to find home
with/in something, someone. Sometimes it happens.
Lesson 2: home can be found.

This too might be lost as we see it lost all around us,
and sometimes we ourselves begin to throw it away
as if home were an unnecessary burden or disposable
clutter in an otherwise unstoppable life.
Lesson 3: home can be lost again.

It takes courage, maybe desperation, to set out again
for home. What we find is a hidden aquifer, our own
unlovable selves carrying the groundwater of home
inside us. But this is hard digging. There was a promise:

"I go to prepare a place for you." Jesus said it and this
I believe is our first obedience – to prepare each day a place
for each other, and for our lovely beloved unlovable selves.
This is the fourth lesson.

(1)

"Spring has returned. The Earth is like a child that knows poems."

Rainer Maria Rilke

Tongan basket c1972

Clearing Catkins

I detect springtime by the sweet-tempered air.
Until now crocus and daffodil have feigned it
in the face of cold winds, even snow.
Today is the real thing. Grand-daughter and I
with rake and broom, without coats,
clear catkins fallen from a pesky alder.

Clara's four, tells me she'd like to go to space –
'but it's crowded, you know, a lot of space ships.'
I argue for un-crowded space. She counters
with examples from Star Trek. I tell her space
           i s   a   v e r y   b i g   p l a c e
She changes the subject
                    to Aladdin,
how he freed the genie; then how she
can tell it's raining by the spots on the bricks.
Yes, I say, and there are other ways.
She agrees to stand very still and yes!
she can *hear* the raindrops, *feel* them!

You're right, grandma, she concedes,
her big red boots still jauntily defiant
on wrong feet and we stay in the rain
til her mother comes because yes,
the real thing is here. Spring.

*Spring rains have freshened
the reflecting pond. Slow splash
from a dripping downspout.*

Yard Guests

The rains have felled
all the forsythia petals.
In their stead, two warblers
blossom yellow
from branch to branch to branch

and two days ago by the little pond,
an Audubon's warbler, tentatively
identified with Peterson's help.
Sweet sojourner, stopping by
for a bite, a breather, a bath.

Stanza

A day is a room
you will never again enter.
Examine its contents lovingly.
White smoke drifting across TV screen;
red kitchen counter I am wiping clean
to receive April's sun; Vatican bells,
their cumbersome mechanism
shown full-screen, ringing, it seems,
out of sync, sending shivers nevertheless;
gatherings of red-robed cardinals
on side balconies, not all smiles; and finally
Il Papa, pontiff, brand-spanking-new
vicar of Christ, his first obedience
first *Benedict*-ion "entrusting himself
to *our* prayers". A nice moment
to click it off, go out and *attend*
to things, pull weeds from gatherings
of upright red-robed tulips outdoing
my fainting daffodils. Near-by traffic
speaks an extraneous language, upstages
the tiny-tongued glass garden-bell
ringing its heart out – urged on
by the always-Holy wind. Are the bells
still ringing in Rome – blessing Urbi et Orbi,
my city, my world this Tuesday
nineteenth of April, year of our Lord
two-thousand and five?

Glass

Floppy tulips in a mason jar
float and hover over the glass table
and the same is reflected
in the deep of the glass, as darkness
was on the face of the deep
the first day, second verse of Genesis,
and the Spirit of God hovered
over the face of the waters
and reflected back to the Father.
There is the face of the deep,
and there is the deep.

Where Paintings Hang

Here, by the red bath tub.
As I settle in for a soak
the red tulips
tell me everything
is possible.

Imagination is a buoyant thing.
Tulips can float, foregrounded,
giant and red against purple landscape.

The painter insisted the picture hung
just like that, outside the bus window,
all the way up the North Thompson valley,
dogging her like the moon.

I Step Outside

I step outside in my plaid pyjamas,
empty the grounds of the French press
into spring's waking garden.
A simple ritual, a good deed atoning
for yesterday's neglectfulness.

Peony Seasons – a glosa* on "In the Time of Peony Blossoming" by Robert Bly

When I come near the red peony flower
I tremble as water does near thunder,
As the well does when the plates of earth move,
Or the tree when fifty birds leave at once . . . Robert Bly

I linger in the back yard
chatting over the fence
while mountains become
indigo silhouettes.
And still, behind the peaks,
the resolute day, like a watchtower
lights the warm June garden.
Suddenly I turn and remember
I've been here, I know this hour
when I come near the red peony flower.

Leaves of peony take on a burnished look,
the wind picks up. Some small twigs
let go their hold and the first frail suicides
begin, yellowed leaves impale themselves
on dry garden stalks, or mix unhealthily
with mildew in the diminishing floribunda.
I cut back my garden visits. Is this a forsaking?
Does God repent his lavish summer spending?
I wonder at photosynthesis put asunder
I tremble as water does near thunder

Now snow covers the cropped peony
and down in a darker world
the roots know their duty
wait and prevail, heedless
of any gardener's plan
to divide, conquer or remove.
Wait, for the stiff earth to stretch
wait, 'til lake-ice cracks
wait, 'til the snow-weight shifts in the grove
as the well does when the plates of earth move.

Spears, dragon-blood red
break through mulch;
the peony joins three dozen daffodils
planted last fall in a burst of faith;
the old apple tree blossoms unerringly
"We come from the dark", they announce.
Quickly we turn our heads to listen,
to hear the wind tremble the tree – the tree
when a thousand leaf buds break out in silence
Or the tree when fifty birds leave at once.

Winged Creatures

Two western tanagers
visit the pond. Alert, energetic,
they flash yellow! orange-red! black!
conscious of their feathered selves
but unselfconscious, quite
unaware they are breath-
stoppingly beautiful

in the eyes of two poets
at the teak dining table
across double glass . . .

. . . who want all those adjectives
to apply to the tiny winged creatures
they are right now releasing
to fly across paper skies.

wisteria god

Gnarly old man reaches
into the alder giving it bloom
gnarly old man threatens
home invasion. Cut him back
keep him trim and pretty
there is altogether too much
cleaving and weeping, too much
falling into everything – blossoms
in my reflecting pool float there
like so many blanched grapes.

This new world

On the white-tiled sill
the white orchid opens.

I and the orchid and the new day,
stilled, at the east window.

In my red and white kitchen I slip
fresh bread into a white toaster

while the orchid floats beside me
in her still white world.

She lays bare her mottled heart
where the bee might suck.

The sky opens wide; everything
waits; somewhere in this new world

the warm new sun is colouring-in
a cowslip's bell.

Poppies, front yard

All the lovely poppies
the tall dreamy poppies
blush pink and orange
in the seductive sunlight
of May's merry month.

All the delectable petals
ruffle and flutter 'round
filaments and anthers.
A festival of fragility
until the next hard rain.

May Evening

It seemed to me the robin singing was the same
the very one who sang when I was twelve, and sad.
Light was leaving the sky as the robin raised her song
to the small commotion already inside of me. A robin
whose calling, it seems, is to solemnize our sadnesses.

I heard the oldness of everything in the robin's song.
In the new-leafed evening, summer seemed to be
coming down a road toward me but I wasn't sure;
nor was I sure of the robin. It could have been, yes
it might have been, the same, the very robin.

Porch light

Night
and the porch light
illuminate the rhododendron.

Rain
has polished all the leaves
polishes still, for they dance a little
under its invisible beat.

Morning
dulls the green, overcasts
the night's promising sight.

Sometimes joy
comes in the night.

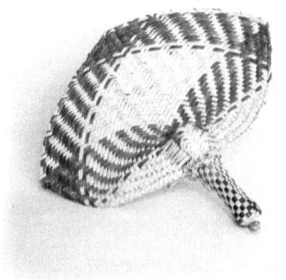

(II)

"all those sleeveless summers"

from the poem *All*

Fijian fan c1972

*shadows
of wisteria leaves flutter
on green shot-taffeta curtains*

*July breeze
through open window
computer screen refreshed*

*gusts of wind
the plastic rattle of Venetian blinds
not from Venice*

The Boy in the Tree

In the back corner of my yard,
wind quickens, an alder sways
calling a boy to run and climb
to ride the rolling air.

The alder holds a pulley
for a line the laundry rides
out to dry in the wind . . .
and sometimes lunch
for the boy in the tree
rides out in a lunch-bag
pinned to the line in the wind.

In the corner of the yard,
there's a boy beguiled in the alder's arms
lured there by love of the wind,
as ocean winds soon will call him
to ride his sail board out from shore.

The boy in the tree
and the boy on the ocean
are the same boy. The one
calls forth the other. And the wind
calls forth the sailor and the climber.

Li-Young Lee, a poet, asks me this . . .
*But wasn't it God
who lured the child ever higher into the tree?*
Li-Young Lee, I speak only of what I am able
to see: the wind and the boy in the tree.

Evenings, after others

Evenings, after others go inside,
I like to keep the conversation going –
an amiable chat with the light.
She agrees to stay.

It's late June and the light is full
of promises: bicycle rides;
somewhere a mountain lake
beginning to warm; laughter
on the patio long into the night.

But she's not all wine and peonies;
she brings up her antithesis – last winter's
long desperate dark.

Not now, I say. Let's picture
a summer afternoon
in a meadow –
yes, with clover
and honey bees.

Summer, she says, has its heartaches,
its forsakings, a summer day opens
the flowers of longing.

Maybe. But for now, I insist,
for this June night, all I want
is this present enchantment;
all I want is to praise you,
sweet lingering light.

O

O Moon
you've come round again.
Not that I doubted you, it's more like
neglect, or simple inattention. A good thing tides
in the affairs of men don't depend on my watchfulness.
O singer with circle mouth – enunciating as if instructed by
the Choirmaster, your minstrelsy breezes through my window,
insistent as passing car radios. Were I truly bent on sleep, I'd
get up and draw the blind, but this conversation has quickened
like caffeine. I'll hear your opinions, philosophy, even. You're
direct – I like that in a friend. I'll quit my angular fretting.
You've shown me reasons to revel. My house has
many windows. I have a good feather pillow.
And tonight you've come
round again.

Bedroom

The edge of the skylight
is the prow of a ship sailing
through rolling white clouds of time.
From my bed below, I make the passage.

A dragon-fly sits on the yellow cedar ceiling,
a sun-dried dragon-fly broach pinned to a bosom.
The cat who doesn't like us is here liking to lie
on our bed. Red geraniums perched on a shelf
reach into the room toward sky light,
drop their paled petals on deep green carpet.

A wire still encircles the cedar beam
where my daughter's white wedding gown
was hung high and handsome – (my wedding dress
years before this room was conceived, or this family).

Water stains on the cedar ceiling show the struggle:
how to make the round roof of this round room
impervious to rain storms. Are we winning?
Sunlight rushes in through the white time-clouds,
illumines every piece of yellow cedar my husband's hands
placed on the ceiling of our round room.

It is too lovely.
I must get up.

Norm dreams himself out of the woods

*Think of a carpenter's dreams. Perfectly mitred
corners, a hammer that sinks a nail with one blow,
drills that sing melodies, saws so fine they divide
cells. There's an even better dream . . .*

*. . . at night in the workshop of the unconscious mind,
the carpenter approaches the day's predicaments.
He dreams a way to cut, fit, angle himself out
of a quandary he was in when he put his tools down
for the day. Morning, he remembers and heads out
to his workshop, into its sawdust materiality.
He puts his dream-solution to the test
and sees it turn out right. All the dream
a worker in wood could want.*

I like a man

who slaps cold water on his face
heads straight out to fetch wood for the heater
     rubs his hands at the thought of a full day.
He'll spend this one in his workshop – teaching himself
to build chairs.
          He'll cut, plane and plan
for his chairs to sit round a mahogany table
in his daughter's city house.
          He might take a break mid-day
make soup from the fridge's vegetable bins
(he's not good with a can-opener) after which
he'll listen to his wife's poetry, try in vain
to say the right thing, then go out
and turn the compost.

He'll attend the hospital exercise program
because his heart doctor said to
though farmers and farmers' sons
don't understand the concept.
Exercise for life?

Life is exercise – when he was young
he loaded hay onto a wagon by pitchfork,
trapped squirrels, sold the pelts. Mornings,
it was out to the dark winter barn
kerosene lantern in hand, pitch hay down
from the shadowy loft, milk a cow or two
before school.
     His father built his own barn.
He builds his own house, eccentric and eclectic
on a suburban lot.
      After open-heart
he still climbs the ladder to clean the gutters.
"Don't worry", some say, "this kind lasts forever"

but I'm not so naïve.
His sons and daughters
will be surprised one day to find themselves
walking over rough ground
discussing suitable gravestones.

dream houses

(1)
. . . I dream houses
empty, imperfectly configured
always I am moving in,
weighing and measuring
the compromises – I'll find a way,
offer kindnesses, give names
to small misshapen rooms:
library, studio, pantry . . .

(2)
. . . in daylight I dream
ample houses: rooms full
of finger painting and flute lessons
porches for philosophy,
alcoves for prayer,
bedrooms playful, honest,
kitchens with wide wooden tables
attics for keeping the past
    nearly out of the way
doors that open easily
    close firmly
plumb walls soundly built
    to keep out the spoilers.
I dream
dream houses . . .

(3)
. . . sometimes in a small nightmare
I inhabit the house of my childhood.
A knock on the door but I can't answer.
I'm on my knees with rags, old towels,
and water coming and coming
in under the kitchen door
inundating, engulfing
and I, sole caretaker
of the old house . . .

(4)
. . . or I approach my childhood home from the south . . .
turn off #3 highway onto gravel road . . . my father's window
white crisscross curtains. The pots of red geraniums
are missing.
        Oh! no-one lives here any more.
One small lamp, left on by some oversight,
gives luminescence to the curtains . . . looking through
I see the barely lighted body of my father
laid out in the south bedroom of our house . . .

(5)
. . . I ask about houses
what I've heard others ask about pets:
when we die, will they be with us in heaven?

Our old fixer-uppers transfigured,
waiting, with rooms full of worlds,
for us to begin moving in . . .

She Comes Into Her Own

All day cliché, cynicism, sophism, cool-ism
work against delight; discomfort her,
lean toward nihilism, everything seeming
plastic or metallic. Then the 5pm bus is all
metal and hot plastic as she slumps her head
on the sill. Riders drain into the depot. Her brain,
groggy, over-heated, is ineffectual in an effort
to empty itself at the end of the line.

She comes into her own dwelling. Cool
terra-cotta tiles ease sweaty feet. Clean,
non-ironic comfort seeps slowly, subliminally
in through extremities. Home's
where you hang out – you and your hat;
where you don't hang yourself out to dry,
she murmurs not noticing her hangover
of cliché. Her humidifier/dehumidifier
(purchase of great price) offers deep
breathing space, reassures as a friend might
(but hasn't of late).

                Her head is clearing
room for reflection. Notions, big ones,
slide in: Body/*versus*/Spirit versus
Body/*and*/Spirit; the likelihood of Time
ever coming to an end; or not. Thoughts click
on pathways implicit in a list of isms
she once visited; her mind opens up theism
versus deism: is or isn't God hanging out,
maybe here, doing whatever it is he does? Possibly
ripening the two tomatoes on the windowsill?

Take your time, girl. No hurry to figure this out.
She runs cold water over curly lettuces, carves
bell peppers into green and yellow parentheses,
slivers a few small commas of purple onion,
then a scatter of cilantro. Oh . . .
                      the lightness
of being allowed slow thinking, no fast pat
answers. Just the slow curving of colour and cool
into the body; the pleasures of dwelling.

More Often – a ghazal*

"If I knew where the good songs come from, I'd go there more often." Leonard Cohen, radio interview:

If I knew, I'd go to that place more often,
where good songs come with grace more often.

You gave me a piano for love of music.
I'll play to enliven our space more often.

You gave me a piano because of our love.
I'll play for the smile on your face more often.

I love when you whistle and sing in the garden.
Sing in your mellow bass more often.

I think I know where the good songs come from.
It's that place where we embrace more often.

You built us a bedroom round and comely.
Take my hand up the staircase more often.

Tomato Vine

I love you coming in
smelling of tomato vine.
I want to taste the ripe
red one you hand me.
The small stems you sometimes
leave attached, I rub between
my fingers. Then I am like you
full of late summer.

In the garden, tiny tendrils
hold on as the vine bears
the burden of flesh, heavy
with sunshine, water and earth.
Staking and tying, your husbanding
lends a hand in their struggle;
your harvesting gladdens our table.

Exchange

He planted a lily bulb.
It bloomed. Its rust-red stamens
brushed his white Tilley hat
as he bent to the garden.
I laundered his Tilley
and set it to dry.
In through my window
blew a lily-scented
August breeze.

Day of Small Things

Who despises the day of small things? Zechariah 4:10

Again this morning, I woke up
alive, so I have another, maybe not
momentous – humdrum will do.

A day of little wind, only a few gusts
of annoyance, a missing sprinkler
and the garden grows thirsty. The sky-blue
hydrangea droops in a sulk. Its name
means water vessel and it wants to be filled.
I'll hand-water. I have time.

In the humdrum house – a fan
oscillates benediction – a priest
sprinkling holy water right and left.
Heat enervates. Only small tasks
will be done (thy will be done
on earth as in heaven.)

Do not despise the day
nor the smallness of things.
Any humdrum day might turn
momentous – someone leaves
and does not return.

Intimations of Grace

When the chickadee rings
the Indian brass bell
suspended from a twisted wisteria
over the small pond where birds
are fond of bathing;

and a butterfly flits frailly
in and out of the light blue
hydrangea, where I sit and read
"Between Noon and Three"
by Robert Farrar Capon and it is,
between noon and three
of a late August afternoon;

when the pinnate shadows
of wisteria leaves rustle
full of grace on terra-cotta tiles;
and the subject of my reading
is the outrage of grace;

and piano music, Chopin,
(live concert from Warsaw)
plays from above the glass patio table,
(speaker well-placed by my husband,
while he lived, loving music);

and in Warsaw, the Polish Chopin
lovers wildly applaud their own;
when the miracle of a jet plane,
flashing overhead, flies away
from itself; and in a small outrage
of grace, someone agrees
to go out in the heat to fetch
French Vanilla ice-cream,

then *"it is meet that we
should make merry, and be glad,
for weren't we all, at some time,
dead and are alive, lost and are found."*

Most of all not water

I wake half-filled
with last night's rain
the drought having broken
while I swam in liquid sleep.
I praise the wet as I've praised
the sun for breaking through
and for its faithful returns.
Do not say the sun is still
and we the ones who circle
and return; nothing is still,
not sun, not earth, most of all
not water. Everything is aquiver.
The birdbath waits, brimming.
My window is open, has been
all night. Nothing is amiss.
A visitor is coming through the rain;
he will come to me wet or dry,
sun or moon, and when I wake
brimming, all will remain
aquiver, though differently.

east-facing

An east-facing kitchen is good
for sleep-crusted eyes, a Strauss waltz
on the radio and across the lane
pink sky peeking between houses.

Hope is a hand placed on your head.
The scales of sleep fall away and you
go out like Saul of Tarsus, baptized
into the first blush of a new sky.

Afternoon In My Kitchen

for grandson *Isaac*, whose name means *laughter*

Isaac, age two
would push a chair
up to the light switch
turn it on, off, on, off
and laugh.

This afternoon from my kitchen window
high wind and the shapes of branches
animate the lawn as light comes, goes,
on, off.
        Someone's tossing clouds
in front of the sun; light and shade
and the shape of Isaac's laughter.

String theory

discovered by spiders
then by children inside
on a rainy day. With string
they join table leg to chair leg
to door knob to drawer pull.
They know everything
is connected, or ought to be
and so they see to their work.

The strings of the wind-chime
disintegrate. Every few months
a slim cylinder on the patio floor,
silvery metal, pock-mocked
by weather. No-one re-strings.
Two chimes remain, a tolling bell
if the wind is strong. I will see to
the purchase of a ball of string.

In morning's slanted rays
I see my back yard held together
by spiders' webs and guy lines.
They quake in the wind
but are not overcome.
The children go outside for the wind
which they love unreservedly.
They run and the spiders catch them,
a surprising, useless prey. Undaunted
the spiders see to their work,
re-fasten the world.

Windowsill

Small white tiles in neat rows on the wide windowsill
of my kitchen – installed by a friendly guy named Tony
who worked enthusiastically while telling me more
about himself than I expected or wanted but it's nice
to have conversation in the middle of a day filled
with housework and little children – speaking of which
he gave my four-year-old five little tiles and told me
"you know what they call me? Tony the Tiger"
and he grinned and I laughed, naive, not getting
what he might be implying, and then his boss
arrived to check on the job, or on Tony, saw the child
playing with tiles and let fly with a lot of Italian
and there was no more chatting as Tony finished up
and I started to think maybe the tiles were a move
to disarm me and the boss knew things but I could be
mistaken about Tony the Tiger since I don't speak Italian
and the tile job was good! For nearly fifty years
those chaste white tiles held fast to my windowsill.

The Glory of the Morning

A small child chants *"morning glory, morning glory"*
the name her mother gave her for the pretty white flowers
clinging and climbing up the old barn boards.

Bindweed! some say, disparagingly;
morning glory, morning glory, says the child.
Inside the barn, her mother milks the Jersey cow.
She loves mornings down at the barn, the sound
of her mother milking, the swoosh in the pail,
loves the sound of words, *morning glory, morning glory*.

An old woman pulls at the vines overrunning her rose bush.
It's their way, she thinks, binding and twining and climbing,
the way they once climbed the old cow barn where she learned
their name, *morning glory, morning glory*. Persistent and tangled,
like memories and the old woman – morning glories, bindweed.
"When did they get such a hold?" *What was I doing all this time?*
All these years of binding and twining. Oh yes, I was living my life.

(III)

"It seems to me sometimes that seasons leave us in the way people do, never just gone, but degree by degree, fading like the smell on a loved one's favourite sweater, until the vanishing one day evolves into memory."

Richard Wagamese

African market basket

*yellow parsnips
in piles on dark soil
the sumac dripping red*

*unrelenting rain
nails November leaves
into concrete sidewalks*

*Low afternoon sun
glares through the hail storm. Crystals
nestle in cold grass.*

Ambulance

The world through my study window:
an ambulance screams down Imperial Street.
Drivers pull over to let life or death have its way
as the low sun this late September day continues
to set maples aglow in what we've always called 'the field'
power line right-of-way, big enough for a good game.
Catch, frisbee. City kids take their fields
where they can find them.

Fifty-plus years in the same house, except for
six months in Montreal and six in Fiji,
and except that it isn't the same house,
it having grown and changed like us
as though it were alive, which it may be.
An ambulance only came the one time
and it wasn't the end. The second one
came for him at our son's house,
already too late.

In the Scattering Season

In the scattering season
what held on so long
lets go.

A squander of leaves
is strewn on the driveway
or lies in ambush on your porch.
Open the door and the brazen rain
comes at you sideways – as the leaves
make their mad dash
across your threshold.

There's no defence.
Everything that holds on
finally scatters.

Cottonwood

On a night with no wind
one large limb of the cottonwood
crackled down to ground.

Daylight – we see what's befallen –
the way you might, in a dream, see a child
fallen so far away you can't reach, can't pull him
back to his feet. From such nightmares
you wake up, though not always.

This limb, once well-connected, now
a wrenched wound, all its juices surfacing,
traumatized leaves twisting into untimely decay.
All week the sharp scent pervades our yard,
passes in through any opening, carries us
to cottonwoods where long ago we carved
words like 'loves' and 'forever'.
Now somehow we must
carry all this away.

Origami

My house-guest, a five-year-old,
folds coloured paper while acquiring
language at an astonishing rate – Japanese
and English. He teaches me origami *and*
his mother-tongue. "In Japanese this is . . . "

For breakfast: nori, rice, vegetables,
sometimes miso soup, nutrition uppermost
in the mind of his Mama. I picture the well-fed
folds of his child brain, the grid laid down,
neurotransmitters going full tilt,
nicely-folding protein.

He's more. His intense focus will often break
for a smile; and one day he slumped down
and cried when the ice-cream parlour closed
just as we arrived; and once he took a square
of red origami paper, cut a simple shape
and gave it to me – a heart.

In my own brain-folds, a memory:
another house-guest, old Japanese Pastor
who rose very early the day of his return
to Japan. In secret he folded many colours,
then went softly into my garden to festoon
my one dracaena with paper cranes.

This gladness remained
framed in my kitchen window as summer
folded into fall. Then the rains came,
and the wind, unfolding, scattering.

Fold, fold again; I meant these words to be
a bright paper bird, but I have no flair
for origami. I cannot find a way
to fold my poem into a pheasant
or a crane, the fledgeling
seems always to falter
though I try to enfold
its palpitating heart
in my palms
gently.

Flicker

November's like this: between storms,
short patches of flickering sun, backyard
leaf-filled fence-to-fence. Wind gusting,
leaves flipping under beaks of at least
a dozen robins. Twice as many juncos.

Birds, leaves – looking like each other.
Short-hop flights. Leaves flip, flap.
The go-go-stop of the birds – as if
they know about *sacred pauses*:
vigilance, deep listening, mystery.

Then comes the red-shafted flicker, flaunting
his stylishness. Sometimes a brief drumming.
Symbiotic exchange: our cedar cladding
for the pleasure of his company.

Now "The City" has come to our lane and felled
the huge cranky cottonwood. Eight hours, a young David
with spurs, ropes, dangling handsaw, chainsaw,
works Goliath down to a stump.

Come spring, no sticky pods, no cotton snow.
Come next November, leaves of the vine maple
minimal and manageable. Will robins and juncos
mine the modest windfall? Will the flicker come?

What the old Japanese Maple Has To Give

This interval of sunshine between November rains
is lucky and the snow shovel works well
for scooping up wet maple leaves.

The young woman walking by for whom I clean
the sidewalk so she won't slip while on her device,
does not look up. The long tall lady from Africa,
(Somalia?) does. Shy hellos from her and her girls.

A friendly chat with a Spanish-accented nanny
while twin red-headed boys sleep in the fancy stroller.
Smiles and Asian nods from two grandparents
shepherding a stroller and each other.

A nice surprise: two teenage guys on skateboards
say hi! Maybe there's a friendly look about me,
having raised skateboarders, nursed the broken bones.

The old Japanese maple is big and leafy and I harvest
a full yard-waste bin of red. I'd rather leave the leaves
glistening and pretty on the sidewalk, but alas,
decaying foliage is slippery and beauty is fleeting. Still
I bring in a few to dry and twinkle on my window sill
until they curl too far into themselves.

Under the Prolific Heavens

Hesitant, intermittent pings. That's rain
making up its mind whether or not to fall
on my skylight. Eventually raindrops
join forces in full downpour, landing
on my ears like a virtuoso drum solo.

Winter, light snowfalls alight on the dome,
leave elegant ephemeral lacework.
Or snowflakes begin surreptitiously
to stitch a heavy coverlet as I sleep.

Seagulls and fall leaves do fly-overs.
Sometimes a satellite slides across.
Always a plane heading out, or into port,
twinkles its position lights, red and green.

Stars too, not as bright as a country night,
but seeable, there beyond the dome,
and the moon, coming and going,
waxing and waning.

And right there, the *Big Dipper*
perfectly framed over the two of us
as we lay down to sleep that first night
under the new dome and the old heavens.

House Beautiful

The wallpaper evokes a meadow – grasses, pale daisies.
Occasional poppies, faded, copy themselves
around the bedroom. In one corner something
is chewing on the poppies, nibbling the daisies.
You had not intended this literal living meadow.
You were thinking House Beautiful,
not House Edible.

        You go away for a day and some live thing
moves into the attic. You turn your head and paint fades;
wood splits behind your back. You return from another
latitude, from lying on hot sand, your house left to its own
devices. You're surprised to see it still standing –
"got away with it this time" – but you know you live
in a falling house, it's only a matter of time;
there is always something gnawing.

House, Grumbling

The crone
croaks her impatience:
"when will she die,
when will the woman leave,
leave me alone
to groan and creak
and die my own death?"

A thousand pairs of eyes,
a thousand pairs of feet,
have passed through,
always pairs, never
a one-eyed man, never
a woman with only one leg,
a few with only one
really good eye or leg.
And this one who lives here
she's no prize, she's falling
apart. When will she go?
The crone rattles her teeth
even on nights with no wind.

Bear's Tooth

I've got one on my windowsill.
Belonged to a friend before he divorced
wife and kids and moved to Missouri.
Killed the bear himself. They
ate the meat, spread the bear grease
on their cowboy boots, had the hide
tanned, nice rug for the house she
designed, they built. When you leave
for Missouri, you're lookin' to come
out of the woods with a new trophy,
so you leave things behind. They say
no-one wins in such affairs but I
got his bear's tooth. It's
on my windowsill.

All

At the end of it all
you know that you know
next to nothing. Confess
your insolvency. Ask for mercy.

Your riches: the enigmatic given
splendid world, the long light
of all those sleeveless summers,
even summer's sere leftovers –
blackening leaves, the brown,
bent grass. Fall's tang, its twinge,
winter, spring, and all in-betweens.

The neighbour's black pickup,
always by the fence, ready
for the brown dog to jump in;
the canny crow in the sumac,
iridescent, annoying. A Steller's jay
flies up inside the cedar. This is how
birds climb trees. They're aliens,
like me, like you.

*Leviticus: "When an alien
lives with you in your land,
do not ill-treat him."
Exodus: "Do not oppress
an alien; you yourselves
know how it feels . . ."*

You go featherless in a world
hilarious with birds; you go plain
in a patterned world – giraffes, zebras,
cheetahs. You limp. What transpires
in the elaborate brain tucked inside
your skull astonishes. Leviticus pops up.
Even so, you know you don't know
all you think you know.
All, even love,
is surprise.

Verily (flashback)

It's hard to escape from self-
imposed captivity – but one day
you're in your little house – pre-renovation,
before the many-windowed cedar house came to be.
You're doing dishes, when a sound penetrates
your familiar desperate reverie. Unfamiliar sound
morphs to familiar. You run to the three-foot square
back porch that juts from your little house, where daily
you lean out to send endless diapers along the clothesline.
Now you lean out and behold! verily!
arriving in the sky, the enigma of departure,
an undulating wedge of geese holding forth
in their raucous celestial voices. Honk,
they say, if you know where you're going.
Honk if you don't. Honk if you love Jesus.
You call to them from your little porch,
'hello, hello!' out loud, and you add
'Bon Voyage' in case they need that
little extra blessing, some courage,
like some of us sometimes do.

Mending Basket

"My housework is so far behind I'm ironing toddlers' clothes and they've all gone off to college."
Phyllis Diller, comedian

'To Do' list: *mend little tear in quilt*
and I thought of all the little tears a quilt
might suffer, rhyming with cares or fears.
Basket piling up with the kind that flow
unresponsive to needle and thread. Those
little tears in the quilt might wait years
for mending, sitting in the basket
like Phyllis Diller's ironing
but not as funny.

How We Finish

May,
and the vine maples laze
in the back corner, seed wings
like sassy red lips saying,
"don't even think of cutting us back."
I confess I am not good
at any kind of cutting back.

September,
and the leaves put on a show:
their full-blown bruises
red/purple, yellow/green.
This is how they finish –
imperfectly, gloriously
bruised, hanging on.

(IV)

"... the cure for permeating cold: submerge hands
and forearms in hot dishwater."

Jolene Nolte, *Winter Evening Ritual*

Rwandan nesting baskets

winter scenes from my study window

winter sun warms
a huddled morning congregation
at the bus stop

chunky chocolate lab
takes my reluctant neighbour
for a bracing walk.

wispy wind blown snow
wet roads, cold bare branches
a purple crocus hiding

A Meditation of Crows

Dull day, midwinter.
Do crows have a to-do list?
Do they scheme and ponder
their opaque lives,
scan their black brains
for inspiration?

Do they wait for divine direction,
perfect and still on the sumac's
curled church pews?

Now they're flexing tail-feathers,
Now they're sidling up to each other.
An infectious caw or two.

Now, all caw. Plea or praise?
The meditation suddenly splits.
The bland blanketed sky
receives the gift, says Hallelujah!
I and the sumac say Amen!

Back Yard, December

After the freeze,
Hydrangea's leaves, blackened,
hang like bats.

One clay pot has cracked.
Found it this morning fallen away,
and two patio tiles, flaky as pie-crust.

Wisteria is old but her remarkable core
continues to fuel grasping tentacles,
insistent extremities.

Through the double-glass window wall
Wisteria's twisted trunk evokes
a woman's entwined thighs.

Touch her, and her bark disintegrates. Now
she and *Hydrangea* are strung with December;
LED lights move through shades of blue,

echo autumn's recolouring
of *Hydrangea*'s fading blooms
to pale rose, to muted mauve.

Bats and blossoms,
stubbornly marcescent, refute
their deciduous nature; refuse

to fall away. I have my own
tenacities. Sticking to this
one house, knowing my own

fairy tales, fiascos, triumphs.
The jokes, the rabbits
pulled from hats.

On December 22, 1999, perigee (the lowest, closest point in the moon's orbit) coincided with full moon and the winter solstice, a fine event to bring in the new millennium.

Moon-Wine

Lights out
        at the supper table
lamb stew
        steaming from dish to mouth
perigee moon
        full and rising
behind black fingers
        of winter trees

In the dark dining room
        pupils dilate
swallowing all
        available light
thirsty to drain
        the bright chalice
and quicken
        our longest night.

Imagine . . .

. . . the mind of humankind
knowing how to hold that jet aloft.
The plane transects a corner of my skylight
just missing the stars of the Dipper's handle.
In this way, morning begins clear, cold, dark,
with me, warm under covers, pondering
intelligent design.

The nearing solstice is countered
by these bright reflective days, sunlight
bouncing off snow, and the soon coming
of Christmas. Such fullness – the moon
three days ago, larger, as they say,
than life. Of course nothing could be.
Always the newest news
and the largest
is life itself.

The moon, waning, promises
return and replenishment.
We name these days Advent,
imagine a coming . . .
. . . in the stark mid-winter of our race.

First Day

When the first day of the year
is seen through the semicircular
bank of windows in your bedroom
and lo, an enchantment
of snow, of snow

and way to the north
the mountains have been turned
upside down while you slept,
their tips dipped in a golden liqueur,
then righted again for you stumbling
from your new year's eve bed
you know, you know

begin to see how
despite wreckages
of the fading year,
despite your own
sins of omission
sins of commission

all shall be well,
and all shall be well,
all manner of thing
shall be well.

Crèche

Putting away the crèche, the grandmother
wraps each worn figure in tissue: the sheep
with its two and a half remaining legs; Joseph,
nose missing; donkey minus an ear; the two
(not three) wise men; the cribbed child
miraculously
intact.

Each year her expectancy, her desire
has bordered on idolatry. Might these
weary plaster forms, fashioned years ago
in another country, purchased cheaply
at a neighbourhood shop, turn
miraculously
into icons

granting glimpses to her and all her issue
of something further in; transforming
mere comforting familiarity into a desire,
an expectancy of visitation, keeping
her faith and theirs
miraculously
intact?

Breakable

Glass shelves in a glass cabinet
carry their weight: wedding gift saucers,
half as many cups; four plates from the 40s;
small vase with birds, from China, chipped rim
turned to the wall; blue and white sake set,
no sake; rice bowl, blue and rust-red, a 'second'
from Arita's ancient pottery kilns; a ceramic
Hakata doll, gift from our favourite home-stay;
serving bowl, deep blue glaze, Kispiox Valley;
old turkey platter from the forfeited farm . . .
          . . . made of earth, hardened by fire,
and by the many weathers of their lives,
these are the ones that made it through.
They carry into age, their iffy-ness,
their several cracks and chips,
their mended places.

Inventory Fragment

"Nothing belongs to me; yet I belong to everything."
Reem Sav See

- seventy-six baskets, no trombones.
- seven picks in a shot glass, no guitar, but
  many strummers and pickers passing through

- one native drum with beater by Cicero August.
- one woven Ahousaht hat by Jessie Webster.
- fourteen fans (anonymous) from far-off places,
  fans that cool you by the twist of your own wrist.

Grand-daughter counted the baskets –
    They came from away; came to stay
    from Africa, Asia, Mexico, the South Seas
- and one from our own north country,
  where a native weaver (name now lost)
  imagined and fashioned it
  ninety years ago.

I'm an accidental collector,
a gatherer, not a hunter,
a receiver of gifts.

Sunset in Real Time

The electrician came today
and all the talk was light,
bulbs, power bars, computers,
extension cords, overloaded
circuits. Now I sit in dark
with only the light of my laptop
and a purple sunset if I look
left, west, the purple is going,
now mostly flaming pink –
inadequate word, pink.
The clouds were purple,
now more beige/grey - that
would be taupe – the colour
of my faded auburn hair. Sunsets
change so quickly, I always
lose the race to the camera.
Not everything is meant to be
recorded – oh! now the sky
under the bank of clouds
is strangely yellow, more
like gold, tinge of orange.

I sense someone's hand
is on the dimmer switch,
though far trees and a building
are still silhouetted. I look away
for a moment – I think the heart
can stand only so much sunset,
only so many sunsets and so
the light must go after all.
Looking west again, the light
is very small. Electric lights
in that single high-rise begin
to stand out from the once-electric
sky now failing, falling away.
The sky has nearly fallen
away, has fallen away, has
fallen. So, the night.

Piano Finally Speaks Her Mind

Place your hand on my frame and you'll know
potential energy awaiting conversion
into kinetic Mozart. Feel me brim and simmer,
strings quivering Scriabin even though
no hammer strikes. Something circles
inside me, a word, a memory. Name it.
The Brahms Intermezzo in A Major
you once brought to light. Now I remember
what I am and why: a gift given
long ago for love. What is it comes
between us. Bring me your sweet fingers,
not fearing the smallness of your gift.

epilogue

*"Houses live and die: there is a time for building
And a time for living and for generation
And a time for the wind to break the loosened pane
And to shake the wainscot . . .*

T. S. Eliot, *Four Quartets - East Coker*

Fijian masi cloth purses

Blue Atlas

He so loved the world
he would spread it open for us
on the dining room table:
world atlas as holy scripture.

See how far, how near, how straight, how winding.
Consider this proximity, that expanse,
the earth's curvature, its great circle flight paths,
the drawn lines between cultures, languages,
latitude, longitude, time zones.

In the South Pacific
the international date line let him travel
into tomorrow and back again
trying to remember which day,
which side of the road to drive on –
according to which power had colonized
Fiji, Tonga, Samoa, New Caledonia,
New Hebrides, the Solomons,
the Gilbert and Ellice Islands.

And in the Atlantic
see how far we flew –
to lonely *Ascension Island*
how far we sailed to *St Helena*
where Napoleon succumbed
to the green wallpaper's poison
and we celebrated in film
his 200th birthday.

Always he returned bearing gifts
to fill our cedar house with bits
of the world. He's many years
gone, and we are vacating,
clearing, clearing.

The blue atlas – how much am I bid
for this master work? How much
for these individual pieces? each map
a thing of beauty when it slipped
from the monthly Geographic into our hands.
Great Peoples of the Past: The Mongols;
The Making of Canada: Prairie Provinces;
The Making of America: Ohio Valley;
Lands of the Bible Today . . .

. . . these documents have landed
in a cardboard box. In our frantic clearing
they've spilled on the study floor, pathetic,
outdated and old as parchment scrolls
to the young who chart their various ways
in paperless territories, new wildernesses.

We are all cartographers, carrying maps
of our own making, our own great circles
in our heads. We try not to lose our way
as we slowly let go the folded paper worlds,
the book-bound worlds, the touchable worlds,
the beloved blue atlas, its blue blue oceans.

Yellow Pages

I've thrown away
the yellow pages, both editions,
I've become a free-run chicken grabbing
pellets of information out of thin air,
zeroes and ones. One small step
at a time, I walk on the moon.
So many lettings-go: mother,
father, brothers, sisters,
husband,
children who turn out to be
part me (and part of me) and part
completely other. I let go of perfection,
which was never mine to hold in any case
but there is always the dream. I let go
of that other century, not forgetting it,
but relinquishing regrets, accepting
with some misgiving, the given
measures of time.

Tragically Hip

An old woman turns up the radio,
hides shoe boxes of ticket stubs
away from helpful down-sizers.
Tristan und Isolde
        in a Roman ruin, Provence;
Mstislav Rostropovich (the fun of pronouncing it)
        Curtis Institute, Philadelphia;
Les Miserables
        New York City New Year's Eve!
        as the ball descended.
If only
she had Tragically Hip final tickets, but no,
too old and tired to go. Gord Downie, living,
even from the beginning had a tinge of dying
in his voice. Finally he stared right at it.

Framing the World

I sat a while to read the room, to see
around the corner for this old house,
its uncounted corners. A spider
in one of them, announced itself.
A wolf spider with eight eyes,
eight windows framing its spider life.
I had already walked the empty rooms
to make a count.
                    My house had many windows
and I wanted to know how many eyes
would be darkened when the day
of demolition came. Such windows,
some grand, some not, some of them
windows to the sky. In all,
I counted Sixty-Six.

The Eye Cannot

The eye cannot bear to gaze upon the permitted violence
of the snarling house-wrecking machine, crazed beast
come to paw, to maul, to un-build, to un-dream a house.

Un Titled

They have taken away my house.
I don't know where they have laid it.
Our house, built by hand, by husbandry,
using that same stardust of which we all
are made – cedar and soil, oak and tile,
birch and brick. Glass for light. Shattered,
it has flown apart. I come apart and will
be scattered. Those who were young there
will slow and grow old. Stars, too, slow
and grow old. My brain will ask "where
is my body?" and I won't know, or "where
is my house" and I will only know to say
"Gone". The place that has known us
knows us no more. I have walked out
the cedar door. I've bought and sold.
What I ask for now is forgiveness,
O One who prepares a place,
O Mender of the World.

The Saffron Gates

Except inside the soul,
Jeanne-Claude and Christo's*
art doesn't linger. Their courage
is in making things to delight
then withdrawing that delight
before delight itself withdraws.

"The Gates" of Central Park
no longer call New Yorkers
to walk beneath them
through rippling saffron panels
shimmering as they did
in the New York light
sixteen days and nights.

Tibetan monks seem to understand;
spend meticulous hours
to make their stunning Sand Mandalas
from colourful ground-up rock.
The intricate patterns then
are care-fully brushed away
for "nothing lasts forever."

Does this help undo the undoing
of a house, show us those rooms
were not heaven's streets
meant for us to tread forever?

. . . it was an imperfectly thrown bowl
imperfectly glazed, imperfectly beautiful
and filled to the eaves with living.
The cedar house,
its many fine sands now brushed away,
its saffron colours still lively
inside our souls.

*there are lovely things in the world that do not
endure, and they're lovelier for that . . .*
remembered line from a movie "Sunset Song"

Lark Ascending

A house well inhabited
opens like a violin well played.
Such aliveness
the guest upon entering
might exclaim "how enchanting"
or one will come
just to curl in a corner to read
A House for Mr. Biswas perhaps
or *The Remains of the Day*
or one might take up pen
to set down reflections,
and another will slowly lower
the needle onto old vinyl
and lingering, listen for
a lark ascending.

"With her foot on the threshold she waited a moment longer in a scene which was vanishing even as she looked, and then, as she moved and took Minta's arm and left the room, it changed, it shaped itself differently; it had become, she knew, giving one last look at it over her shoulder, already the past."

Virginia Woolf, *To the Lighthouse*

*Notes and Acknowledgements

1. *Cedar, First Light* – *Bukwus – also known as the Wild Man of the Woods, is a supernatural creature from the Kwakwaka'wakw Nation. I have not been able to identify the carver of this plain cedar mask. My husband knew but did not write it down and now he's gone. There is no signature on the piece. Thank you to the anonymous carver.

2. *I am* – *Indian Horse* a novel by Richard Wagamese.

3. *Old Saying* – *Petra*, poem by John William Burgon, last line of his poem is "a rose-red city half as old as time."

4. *Stanza* – Stanza in Italian means "room" or "stopping place" or "guest room".

5. *Peony Seasons* – *Glosa definition – The glosa is an early Renaissance form developed by poets of the Spanish court in the 14th and 15th centuries. In a glosa, tribute is paid to another poet. The opening quatrain, called a cabeza, is by another poet, and each of its four lines is imbedded elsewhere in the glosa.

6. *This New World* – "Where the bee sucks, there suck I, in a cowslip's bell I lie." Wm. Shakespeare.

7. *Porch Light* – "Weeping may endure for a night, but joy comes in the morning" (Psalm 30:5).

8. *The Boy in the Tree* – Italicized lines are from *God Seeks A Destiny* by Li-Young Lee, American poet.

9. *Evenings, after others* – Using William Stafford's first line: "Evenings, after others go inside" from his poem, *All the Time*.

10. *More Often* – *Ghazal – traditionally invoking melancholy, love, longing, and metaphysical questions, ghazals are often sung by Iranian, Indian, and Pakistani musicians. Its form is a chain of couplets with repeating rhymes.

11. *Most of all not water* – Prompted by part of a line "half-filled with last nights rain" from the poem *Plume* by Dorianne Laux.

12. *east-facing* – See the conversion story of St. Paul (Saul of Tarsus) in the New Testament, Acts 9.

13. *First Day* – Italicized quote from Julian of Norwich [1342–1416].

14. *The Saffron Gates* – Re Jeanne-Claude and Christo* see: https://christojeanneclaude.net/projects/the-gates May 31, 2020, Christo died at his home in New York, age 84.

15. *Lark Ascending* – *A House for Mr. Biswas*, a novel by V. S. Naipal; *Remains of the Day*, a novel by Kazuo Ishiguro; *The Lark Ascending*, a tone poem by Ralph von Williams.

Previously Published

Most of all not water – Previously published in *WordWorks* Winter 2015 (Federation of B.C. Writers).

Intimations of Grace – Previously published in *Silence, The Breaking Of It* 2013 Big Tree Publishing.

Day of Small Things – Previously published in *Silence, The Breaking Of It* 2013.

She Comes Into Her Own – Previously published in *Silence, The Breaking Of It* 2013.

Piano Finally Speaks Her Mind – Previously published in *Celebrating Poets Over 70*. ed. M. F. Vespry and E. B. Ryan, Tower Poetry Society.

A number of the poems in this book have appeared in self-published chap books.

Thank you . . .

- To my children and their spouses and all the grandchildren whom I love beyond measure . . . thank you for loving the Cedar House and me and for helping me through it all.
- Big Tree Publishing (Russ Rosen) for getting the book out.
- Patty Nelson for designing my book with skill, understanding and patience.
- Diane Tucker and Barb Kobabe for reading and critiquing my manuscript.
- Cheryl Bear and Melaney Gleeson-Lyall for reading and commenting.
- Richard Osler for his watchful eye as he read my manuscript, and for his generous and insightful remarks (see back cover).
- Braden Olson and Ben Rosen-Purcell for photos.
- Writers Sue Braid and Liz McNally for being listening friends.
- My sister, Jean Higashi, who regularly came to the Cedar House for tea (normal tea please, not that fancy herbal stuff).
- Honeymoon Bay retreat poets, other poetry groups, who've helped me improve my writing by their knowledge and love of poetry and their diverse voices.
- A special note of thanks to the late Patrick Lane and to Lorna Crozier for the gift of their brilliant, inspired teaching at retreats – which I've attended yearly from 2009 to the present.

www.ingramcontent.com/pod-product-compliance
Lightning Source LLC
Chambersburg PA
CBHW021449070526
44577CB00002B/325